Survivor Guide
for
STUDENT
SUCCESS

8F's

Every student needs for a 4.0 in LIFE

Earl C. Johnson

Survivor Guide for Student Success
8 F's Every Student Needs for a 4.0 in Life

Earl C. Johnson

Copyright © 2007 Earl C. Johnson

Contact:
Earl C. Johnson
P.O. Box 12723
Seattle, WA 98111

Printed in the United States of America

ISBN: 978-1-4992-2259-3

*This book is dedicated to
the human spirit...*

and the student in all of us.

Contents

Survivor Guide
for
STUDENT
SUCCESS

A Message to you, the STUDENT!

It is for you, the student, that I have assembled this Survivor Guide. It is not about surviving or survival. Rather this book seeks to offer you the opportunity to benefit from the life altering experience of a Survivor.

In the process you will hopefully gain insight into, and further understanding of this adventure we call life. It is my wish that each of you find at least one thing within these pages that makes a difference in your life. A Survivor often looks to answer the question "why me?" and you will be helping me do just that by benefiting from the Survivor Guide. Take what you learn here and apply it. You will be on your way to creating for yourself, a life rich in meaning, stronger in purpose and more rewarding than your wildest dreams.

> "What is the use of living, if it be not to strive for noble causes and to make this muddled world a better place to live in after we are gone?"
>
> *Winston Churchill*

Survivor Guide

for

STUDENT
SUCCESS

My Name Is Earl

Hello, my name is Earl Johnson. I am a 9/11 World Trade Center survivor from the 51st floor of the North Tower. Let me take a moment to tell you a little bit about myself before you move onto the rest of this book.

It is my Mission in life to offer students just like yourself, the benefit of my experience that day so that you may use it for good in your own life and the lives of those that your path will cross. It hasn't always been that way.

My background includes a Bachelors degree in Economics from the University of Washington and a twenty eight year career in the Financial Services industry. I have held positions that included President and CEO, Senior Vice President and Managing Director, with enterprises ranging from start up's to large, diversified financial services corporations.

I have also worked as a paperboy, babysitter, gardener, day laborer, factory worker, machinist, ski instructor and STUDENT!!!

Somewhere along the way while in the latter capacity, I, like you, faced the often daunting challenge of successfully multi-tasking a rigorous academic schedule, a demanding social life and confusing thoughts about who others thought I should be and what I really wanted for myself.

In the end it has all worked out fine as I am sure it will for you. That is not to say that there haven't been significant ups and downs, setbacks and the occasional outright failure along the way. Each step however has ultimately left me with a greater appreciation for this journey we call life, and a willingness to forge ahead and discover what lies down the road and around the next bend.

I enjoy a great life, I am blessed with a loving family and friends, and pursue my passion for speaking to young and old alike. The Pacific Northwest is where I was raised and feel most at home. Please feel free to contact me at:

Earl@911survivorstory.com

*"Other things may change us,
but we start and end with family."*
Anthony Brandt

Family

Family was specifically chosen as the first of the **8 F's EVERY STUDENT NEEDS** because it is the one thing we all have in common. Additionally, it is a topic that facilitates an initial discussion of several key concepts.

The first has to do with how you see things; in this case the perception you hold about your family.

> "If you ever start feeling like you have the goofiest, craziest, most dysfunctional family in the world, all you have to do is go to a state fair. Because after five minutes at the fair, you'll be going 'you know, we're all right. We are dang near royalty.'"
>
> *Jeff Foxworthy*

Does this sound vaguely familiar? It should because it applies to almost everyone. The test is whether or not you smiled or laughed when you read that. If so, welcome to the club. The fact that so many students can relate to this is one of the world's greatest equalizers in that it cuts across economic, social, racial and geographic boundaries so completely and in so many different ways.

The second concept is about the reality of your family, good or bad, and the importance of, and value found in, recognizing that while we don't choose who our family is, we completely control how we participate as an individual member. This raises the issue of empowerment, a central component of your life not just as a student, but ongoing throughout life in general. You decide; you have control over how you relate and interact with your family members just as you will with for example, coworkers in the future. Will you be a negative force, that emotional tornado that rips through family relationships with little concern or awareness for others and their needs and feelings while you focus solely on yourself, or will you chose to be a compassionate, caring "member" of something much larger than yourself?

Family can be so much more than simply blood relations. That by definition is the lowest common denominator. It takes energy, effort, desire and sacrifice by each member to make a family more than simply genetic branches of a family tree. To help you put this into practice and hopefully make it real for you, I want to address the issue of Family from a time line perspective with two reference points; your past, and your future.

At the "your past" stop on our time line, we will find the reality of your family environment, the one you know and have lived with up to now. For simplicity, but at the risk of seeming insensitive, I have just three categories for you to describe your family environments here in your past. They are: the Good; the Bad; and the Ugly.

For those of you fortunate enough to place your family experience to date in the Good category, congratulations. You have been blessed and have been given a great starting point in life. Be grateful and aware of your gift so that you may continue to enjoy and nurture its fruits. Is there anyone you can think of that would benefit or appreciate hearing your perception on this topic? Give them a call or send an email and make their day!!!

To those of you who put your family experience thus far in the Bad category, spend some time reviewing your contributions to that environment and be willing to accept responsibility for any actions in your past that may have been a contributing factor to your category selection. Be courageous and if possible communicate your thoughts to other family members. If done right, with respect and honesty, you may be surprised how they respond with their own thoughts, feelings and reflections of mistakes they made, in an effort to match your expressions of self discovery.

Now the hard part. I hope that very few of you felt it necessary to select the Ugly descriptor, but I know you're out there. A fact of life today is that many families suffer from the effects of drug and alcohol abuse, extreme poverty and a dangerous environment where every day brings yet another problem without a solution. The evils of physical and mental abuse, domestic violence and sexual assault are all too often an unfortunate part of many students' family environments. I am not a professional counselor, nor qualified to guide you with any real expertise, but I can offer you this; This Guide is for you. Everything I want to say in these pages is my gift to you. You have been dealt a lousy hand to start life, but you can and will survive it! Better yet, you can empower yourself to thrive and build a better life and future all your own. The first and best way to do that is by empowering yourself and staying a student! Get your education and give yourself the gift that will last a lifetime.

***If you don't have family resources the next "F" you need is
for Friends, as they are the family YOU get to choose.***

Let's move on to the next reference point on our time line;
your future. Again, one of the common themes throughout
this Guide is the belief that each of us as individual's, has the
power to change. Change ourselves, the way we act or how
we react, change our environment, change our relationships.
Of course we must not only want to change, we must take
action to change. The slang term "wannabe" highlights this
perfectly. We all want to be …. something, somebody, but it
is our ACTIONS that will create this for us, not simply our
desires. Desire is a part of it but by itself is not enough to
make our dreams real. You must take action !!!

Specifically with regard to Families, we are limited in that we
can't change who our Family is comprised of, but we certain-
ly can change how we participate as an individual member.
If you believe that making positive changes in your future
family relationships would be a good thing, then by all means
don't waste another minute. Use the worksheet on the next
page to help you focus and follow through.

Family
Action Step Worksheet

List three things **you want to**
change or improve with your Family :

_____

_____

_____

List three things **you will do** to
make the elements above a reality:

_____

_____

_____

*"Friendship is the only cement
that will ever hold the world together."*
Woodrow Wilson

Friends

Friends was the natural choice for the second of the **8 F's EVERY STUDENT NEEDS**, in that the basic concept of a friend can be considered a bridge of sorts, connecting between our family, ourselves and the rest of the world. The development of friendships and the changing nature of their relative importance throughout our lives can be seen as the result of our efforts to fill the void created naturally as we first prepare for, and then ultimately experience, a life beyond our parents and the environment we were raised in.

This bridge or link we call friendship between ourselves and others that we meet in life is not a one size fits all. In fact it comes in different shapes and sizes; it is built with a number of different materials, some weak and some stronger than steel; it is as often left unfinished and abandoned, as it is completed and given regular maintenance.

My purpose here is to illustrate and discuss these differences so that you, the Student, will be better prepared to build a few strong bridges that will serve you well and stand the test of time.

Let's start with a simple question.

What is Friendship? Now that may sound like a silly question but when we really try to answer it we get a lot closer to both seeing and understanding the key things that make a good friend from both our own point of view and the perspective of others.

Consider the following:

> "Friendship with oneself is all-important, because without it one cannot be friends with anyone else in the world."
>
> *Eleanor Roosevelt*

When I came across this quotation, I knew that I wanted to use it right here, at the beginning of the discussion about Friends. The concept it addresses is so true, so obvious, we often look right past it when we are trying to solve friendship questions in our lives. Not that it is the root problem in all cases, but it is a great place to start looking and satisfy ourselves that a friendship problem we are dealing with does not stem from within.

Friendship is not the only topic that this applies to as well. I think you could fairly say that in general, we as individuals are better prepared and poised to succeed in life and the world at large, if we are first happy and at peace within ourselves. If you are not ready to make that claim, it will be much more difficult and more challenging to provide the necessary attributes for good relationships with others. You must like yourself on the inside, before you can expect others to do the same. Be honest with yourself, and if you find things you wish to change, do it. Start right now, take action, ask for help, in essence do whatever is necessary to make the changes you desire. You CAN do it and you've already done the hard part by identifying a change is both necessary and what you want.

Another key defining characteristic of Friends is the twin concepts of Loyalty and Trust. Remember always that Trust is built and Loyalty is given. The dynamic interrelationship between these two critical friendship components is powerful and deserves to be clearly understood.

Trust can be considered the measure of strength between Friends. The more trust, the stronger the relationship. How do you build Trust in a relationship? Over time, and with great attention to being supportive and caring as to the other parties feelings, emotional needs and most of all, being willing to share each others private feelings and personal successes and failures without judgment or ridicule.

Loyalty is often a source of significant disruption in developing friendships. I believe this stems from an incorrect perception or misunderstanding of where loyalty comes from. You have probably heard someone say "you haven't earned my loyalty" or thought yourself "loyalty has to be earned". This point of view see's loyalty as something to be "purchased" by some amount of effort, good deeds, or other action. You can't earn or buy someone's loyalty. It is something that people choose to give to you. Being a loyal friend, standing up for someone even when you think they're wrong, can be one of the greatest gifts one friend can give to another.

Forgiveness is another of the **8 F'S EVERY STUDENT NEEDS** and a topic of another Chapter, but it has been said that forgiveness is loyalty in action. Just as you can't make someone forgive you, you will be frustrated and unsuccessful with friendships that you measure by your perception of whether or not they have earned you loyalty. In these situations it would be better to ask yourself, what can I do to show my loyalty to the other person?

"The glory of friendship is not the out-stretched hand, nor the kindly smile nor the joy of companionship; it is the spiritual inspiration that comes to one when they discover that someone else believes in them and is willing to trust them."

Ralph Waldo Emerson

I'm sure that each of you can quickly identify multiple people in your life that fit in each of the categories identified on the following diagram.

Types of Friends

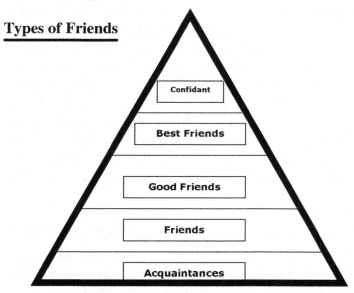

Confidant

Best Friends

Good Friends

Friends

Acquaintances

Just for fun, let's turn things around. Where in the pyramid would you think that each of those individuals you've identified, place you from their point of view? Are you a mere acquaintance, good friend or a trusted confidant in their eyes? Does your experience of interaction with each of these people match your choice for them and them for you? This is not particularly important at the beginning levels of friendship as it may simply result from a slightly different definition of acquaintance vs. friend or friend vs. good friend. However, as you move upward towards the best friend and confidant levels, it becomes increasingly more likely that each of you will view the other in a similar role. Why is this?

One key reason is that over time as we accumulate experiences with a friend or acquaintance, each of us subconsciously makes a judgment as to the other person's responses, actions or the lack thereof, in a wide variety of circumstances. As we build our "experience database" with a particular person, we begin to summarize our information, develop our opinion and assign a general category of friendship to this individual.

> "Be courteous to all, but intimate with few, and let those few be well tried before you give them your confidence. True friendship is a plant of slow growth, and must undergo and withstand the shocks of adversity before it is entitled to the appellation."
>
> *George Washingon*

Of course with the passage of time and the benefit of more inter-action with the person, we will continuously update our view and as a result, most people experience a natural ebb and flow of their friend based relationships. Someone who seems extremely important to us in our lives at one point, may with the passage of time and distance, move into an inactive role. These types of friends reside in what I call the Friendship Bank. A storage place of sorts, filled with deposits of good-will and friendship with people whom we have crossed paths with in life. We can never know when someone will re-appear in our lives, out of the past and perhaps for only a fleeting moment. But if at our last encounter, we were friends of any kind, the least we will experience is a warm and pleasant feeling, a familiarity and sincere appreciation for the opportunity to say hello to an old friend.

> "Truly great friends are hard to find,
> difficult to leave, and impossible to forget."
>
> *G. Randolf*

Be an unforgettable FRIEND !!!

PS. You may have noticed I didn't discuss that class of "friends" we all have known: the users, the moochers, the opportunists, the selfish and self centered, the fair-weather types that never seem to be there when it really counts and always there when there's something in it for them. My purpose in not specifically addressing these folks was to make the point, you don't need them, don't want them, and most importantly you don't want to let them drag you down and distract you from being the best you can be. Enough said!

Friends
Action Step Worksheet

List three people **you want to**
change or improve your Friendship with:

_____

_____

_____

List three things **you will do** to
change the Friendships listed above:

_____

_____

_____

"Failure should be our teacher, not our undertaker. Failure is delay, not defeat. It is a temporary detour, not a dead end. Failure is something we can avoid only by saying nothing, doing nothing, and being nothing."

Denis Waitley

Failure

Failure is the next "biggy" of the **8 F's EVERY STUDENT NEEDS**, ranking just after Family and Friends. You may be asking yourself, "why failure? What is this guy talking about? I don't want failure in my life, let alone need it. In fact, I already have too much failure!" Before you toss this book and turn your attention to something else, read the quote again on the opposing page, and then again, ONE MORE TIME !

Ok, it's clear then, we cannot avoid failure. It is as much a part of life as breathing, eating, and sleeping. Why I want to address it here is the important question. Specifically, this chapter covers your ability to understand failure. The role failure needs to play in your life, and the absolute "must have" set of skills you need to squeeze the maximum amount of benefit from each and every failure that occurs.

Perhaps the best way to get started is to take a half step backward and consider for a moment that failure is only one of two possible outcomes, the other of course being success. Success and failure are simply the two possible results we can achieve when trying to accomplish something. That something can be anything at all. You can think of them as the opposite sides of the same coin. Of course I'm looking to discuss significant goals you will set or objectives you will seek and not trivial, everyday life things like failing at taking out the trash for your Mom or missing a spot when you wash your car.

For our purpose here, it may be useful to think of failure as adversity. The fact that you failed at something may itself be the adversity you're facing; or the adversity may have presented itself first, and you have not yet determined whether you will succeed or fail in overcoming this obstacle in your life. It doesn't matter which it is. The prescription for what you need to do is the same in either case and it all starts with **ATTITUDE**.

> "Courage is going from failure to failure
> without losing enthusiasm."
>
> *Winston Churchill*

Controlling how we let ourselves feel when we fail or face some adversity is critical. Do you know why failure feels so bad? It is primarily because we internalize it, take it personally and actually let it effect how we feel about ourselves in our own mind! If we let it, failure can negatively impact our ego and sense of identity as we often experience feelings of inadequacy, ineffectiveness or even isolation. In addition, these feelings are all magnified in intensity if we are not prepared to see failure as a common occurrence and let it catch us off guard.

If instead, you responded to failure with the attitude of learning what you could from it and then moving on, you could skip the whole "pity party". Take the view that this failure was simply another stepping stone toward success and get moving again. This of course takes a special quality in a person, and that is COURAGE. So be courageous, take failure in stride, keep your head up and your feet moving as you head down life's road.

> "Patience and perseverance have a magical effect before which difficulties disappear and obstacles vanish."
>
> *John Quincy Adams*

On a personal note, I want to take this opportunity to share with you my perspective on this topic that is a direct result of my survival on 9/11. I believe that by embracing adversity and failure; by seeing obstacles not as road blocks, but as opportunities; and failures not as endings but as simply another step toward success, I have found clarity in my life that was not present before 9/11. It goes something like this.

Life Is Filled With Adversity And Failure… Living Is The Process Of Overcoming Them.

The reality of September 11, 2001 has challenged all Americans to find within themselves a mechanism for healing and understanding. Perhaps the silver lining that can be found in that most horrific of days is the fact that many millions of Americans, in the process of grieving for those lost that day and the loved ones they left behind, have learned something about adversity that can have a positive impact on their own lives and unique circumstances. You see, I believe that in order to truly be successful in life, to push the envelope of what we can achieve, we must condition ourselves to expect and accept adversity and failure, and not shy away from them. I would even go so far as to argue that if you face no adversity, if you don't experience any failure in your life, you're not really living; you're just existing.

21

None of the truly valuable things worth having in life are achieved without overcoming adversity and failure many times and in many different ways. Things like a loving family, lifelong friends, a vocation you're passionate about and a community in which you're proud to be a part of. So I challenge you to not fear failure, rather embrace it! In doing so, you will ignite and unleash all your God given talents in the quest to overcome it, whatever IT may be.

Are there any guarantees? NO !

Will you always be successful? NO !

Will things always work out the way you want
or intend them to? NO !

> "Men succeed when they realize that their failures are the preparation for their victories."
> *Ralph Waldo Emerson*

What I can guarantee you is that by not seeing failure as a natural part of life and something to accept, learn from and move on; by not seeing obstacles and adversity in your life as opportunities, you will be limiting your potential in life, the lives of those closest to you, and yes even the lives of strangers whom your path crosses in life.

> "There is no failure except in no longer trying. There is no defeat except from within, no really insurmountable barrier save our own inherent weakness of purpose."
>
> *Ken Hubbard*

Not expecting and accepting failure with courage, patience and persistence is to accept defeat from life's obstacles. I say bring it on. The question is, what do you say?

Failure
Action Step Worksheet

List your three biggest Failures and what you learned:

_____

_____

_____

List three things **you will do** to change
how you react to Failure in the future:

_____

_____

_____

"Forgiveness is freeing up and putting to better use the energy once consumed by holding grudges, harboring resentments, and nursing unhealed wounds."

Sidney & Suzanne Simon

Forgiveness

Forgiveness is perhaps the most important of the **8 F's EVERY STUDENT NEEDS**, because it is something we need to learn how to do for others as well as ourselves. Forgiveness can be described as the mental, emotional and or spiritual process of healing yourself from some wrongdoing or inequity that you have suffered. The terms "letting go" or "let it go" are often used to describe the process of forgiveness as we attempt to end our feelings of anger or resentment toward a person or persons who we hold accountable for the pain we feel. Each and every one of us has been on the receiving end at some point in our life of an injustice or inequity, something that just wasn't fair. Well, at the risk of sounding like a parent, LIFE IS NOT ALWAYS FAIR. LIFE IS NOT ALWAYS KIND. Therefore, it is critical to your success and happiness in life that you understand how to harness the power found in forgiveness and the real need to make the act of forgiving a familiar and practical part of your life.

> "Life is an adventure in Forgiveness."
>
> *Norman Cousins*

There are two views of forgiveness, one where it is considered a gift that you give and the other where it is something that needs to be purchased or bought by others through various acts of repentance like a good apology or the completion of some punishment. I believe you will be better off viewing Forgiveness as a gift you give to others rather than expecting others to "buy" it from you. What if they don't want to, don't care, or worse, are unaware of their actions negative impact on you and don't therefore even suspect they may need to apologize or ask forgiveness? Do you really think people who you believe have hurt you in the past are wasting any of their time thinking about you right now? Of course not. So why should you spend any of your valuable time and life energy thinking about them? Take the wheel and drive!! Give the gift of forgiveness to someone who has hurt you. You will be amazed when you realize it was really a gift you gave to yourself!

> "There is no weakness in Forgiveness."
> *Joel Osteen*

And speaking of yourself, maybe the person whom you really need to forgive the most is the one you see in the mirror every morning. Yes, that's right, I mean you. Have you ever considered for a moment that the one person in your life that needs and deserves your forgiveness the most is YOU ? Accepting the fact that we are human and thus imperfect can require first forgiving oneself for our imperfections and freeing ourselves from the delusion that we can ever attain anything close to perfection in this life. Sure, there is that opportunity in specific areas but not in life overall. We can bowl or pitch a perfect game, play par golf, make the perfect cappuccino and even get that brass ring of a 4.0 grade average, but as we saw in the last chapter, these successes were likely preceded by many, many failures. If we are unable to forgive our failings, it is likely we will never accomplish anything of significance in our life. Forgiving after all means your willing to accept the mistake, even if it's yours, look past it, let bygones be bygones and MOVE ON!

> "I will never allow another man to shrink my soul by making me, hate him."
>
> *Sachel Page*

On the other hand, failure to forgive is a life sentence you hang on yourself. The accumulation of anger, resentment and hurt that would accompany a life without forgiveness is an unbearable burden. Many of the unhappy people you meet in life are experiencing this very thing; the inability to move on, to forgive a hurt inflicted by another, to simply and completely let it go. A verse from a beautiful song says it all:

> "There are people in your life who've come and gone. They let you down and hurt your pride. Better put it all behind you; life goes on. You keep carrying that anger, it'll eat you up inside."
>
> *Don Henley*

Understanding the consequences of not being able to embrace forgiveness in your life is an important first step in putting the power of forgiveness to work for you. Equally important is your ability to understand why, when we give the gift of forgiveness, we often stop short of the ultimate goal of forgiving and forgetting. There are primarily two issues at work when this is the case. First, you believe that if you continue to remember what was done to or against you, that this will somehow ensure that the offending party will also remember how badly you were hurt and in some way punish them. WRONG! That is like taking a poison pill and expecting the other person to get sick! Secondly, we let ourselves buy into the illusion that our remembering of the event will somehow help create a protective barrier around us and help avoid further hurt in the future. Also WRONG ! Only by seeing the hurtful acts of others toward us as something outside of our control can we free ourselves to exercise the choice to forgive and forget. You can't stop people from hurting you in the first place. You can only choose whether or not you will let it repeat itself over and over by failing to find a path to forgiveness and forgetting.

> "Forgiveness is the key to
> action and freedom."
>
> *Hannah Arendt*

Forgiveness
Action Step Worksheet

List three people you need to Forgive:

_____

_____

_____

Describe what **you will do** to
Forgive more freely in the future:

_____

_____

_____

"Without faith, nothing is possible.
With it, nothing is impossible."
Mary McLeod Bethune

Faith

Faith is the next of the **8 F'S EVERY STUDENT NEEDS**. Let me state right here, at the beginning of this Chapter that it is not my intention to provide you with a religious based discussion of Faith. I am a Christian, you may be also, or Jewish, or Morman or Buddist, or Muslim, or Atheist, or Wicken, or whatever. It is not my focus here.

The faith that I want you to focus on here in the Survivor Guide for Student Success is of the most personal kind; the faith that you have in yourself. Your ability to believe in yourself and your ability to define your dreams and make them as real for you as the air you breathe. The quotation on the opposing page is so true. Without faith in yourself and your abilities, whatever they may be, life will be a real struggle. With it, you will find yourself going further and achieving what those without such faith would call impossible. The US Marine Corp. has a saying "the difficult we do immediately, the impossible takes a little longer." Wouldn't it be great if we all got out of bed each morning with that degree of faith in ourselves? I'll make you a deal; I'll promise to say those very words each morning if you will make the same pledge, right here, right now.

> "We must not, in trying to think about how we make a big difference, ignore the small daily differences we can make which, over time, add up to big differences that we often cannot foresee."
>
> *Marian Write Edelman*

Could it really be that easy? Recite a few words and presto… my dreams come true? Of course not, but the point here is that you are engaging in what is called "positive self speak", and it is a great habit to form. Most successful people practice it in one form or another and you should too!

In addition, engaging in this positive behavior should help increase your awareness of the things you say to yourself in general. We all do it, mostly out of habit and mostly with a negative message. We learn this self-destructive behavior by usually first hearing those negative messages from others, but then internalize them and make them our own. Some examples should help make this clearer for you. You might have heard someone say to you "You'll never make it to college" or "Your not good enough to" _____ (fill in the blank), or "You don't have what it takes to be" _____. I bet that these or other comments like them are rattling around somewhere in your subconscious. You must reprogram the message your hearing within yourself from one of negativity and self doubt, to a positive one based on faith in yourself and a belief in your abilities. Simple examples would be "I believe in me" or "I know that I can do it" That is the path to your successful future. That is what you need to do in order to reach your goals, enjoy a great life, find happiness and generally achieve your full potential.

> "All the strength and force of man comes from his faith in things unseen. He who believes is strong; he who doubts is weak. Strong convictions precede great actions."
>
> *James Freeman Clarke*

It has been my experience in life thus far that personal faith is something that can often wait in reserve and is available to be called upon when I have failed in some significant way. I have also observed that in these instances it is more powerful when mixed with courage and blended with the input and love from the first two of the 8F's Family and Friends. It is faster acting when I can apply the lessons we have covered in F's 3 & 4, Failure and Forgiveness. At this point, I hope you are all gaining a sense of the connections between these first five chapters. Keep and nuture faith in yourself and remember, it's easy to be good, it takes courage to be great.

Go be GREAT !!

F # 5

Faith
Action Step Worksheet

List three ways you show Faith in yourself:

_____

_____

_____

List three things **you will do** to
have more Faith in yourself:

_____

_____

_____

"Everything can be taken from a man but the last of the human freedoms...to choose one's attitude in any given circumstance, to choose one's own way."

Victor Frankl
Holocaust Survivor

Freedom

Freedom follows Faith as the next of the **8 F'S EVERY STUDENT NEEDS**. As a general topic, Freedom can be discussed from a great many different perspectives. Our focus here in the Survivor Guide for Student Success will be primarily on the freedom you already possess to determine your own path in life. I will also offer you the opportunity to examine freedom from a broader perspective that will hopefully help you to better understand the world in which you are part of. By providing you these two perspectives, it is my desire to help you grasp the powerful but simple truth that you as an individual, free to choose your own path in life and empowered with knowledge through education, can make a significant contribution to the world in general through positively impacting the lives of countless others.

> "We must not believe the many, who say that only free people ought to be educated, but we should rather believe the philosophers who say that only the educated are free."
>
> *Epictetus*

If you haven't realized it yet, you live in an age where the value of knowledge has never been greater. We are witnessing daily, through the realities of global markets, worldwide instantaneous communication and historically liberal, free flows of capital, goods and services between nations, that the opportunities for the under-educated among us are indeed, significantly limited as compared to previous generations.

Traditional job opportunities once plentiful for those without formal education (ie High School or College diplomas) have moved offshore to developing countries like India, China and Indonesia with vastly greater numbers of under-educated, cheaper laborers. At the same time, competition from the educated class of these very same countries, have raised the bar for you as their members seek opportunities to gain employment here in America.

> "Freedom begins between the ears."
>
> *Edward Abbey*

My point here is not to bore you to death with a discourse on global macro economics, but merely point out that your generation and those that will follow you will, during your lifetime, be presented with the continual challenge of a need to learn. In other words to periodically upgrade your internal, central processing unit! Education is not just something for the young. It is something you should be preparing yourself to both enjoy and engage in throughout your life. The knowledge base of mankind has never expanded so rapidly. At the same time, the opportunities to participate in its expansion and enjoy its benefits have never been so freely available. But neither has the risk been so great, or the cost so high, of failing to recognize early in life, the inherent value and necessity in attaining a love of learning and a lifelong thirst for knowledge. Never forget that inside each of you is the power and the freedom to determine your own degree of participation along the path of success in life. Never let anyone tell you otherwise; and most importantly, never ever let life challenges cause you to doubt your ability to learn, adapt and pursue your dreams.

> "Our contest is not only whether we ourselves
> shall be free, but whether there shall be left
> to mankind an asylum on earth for civil and
> religious liberty."
>
> *Samuel Adams*

I would be completely remiss in my duties as a 9/11 Survivor addressing the topic of Freedom if I did not spend a few minutes discussing the topic from the global political perspective and offer you my thoughts on the role your generation, and you, as an individual, will play in the world you are about to inherit.

> "The wave of the future is not the conquest
> of the world by a single dogmatic creed, but
> the liberation of the diverse energies of free
> nations and free men."
>
> *John F. Kennedy*

Of course the dogma that JFK was referring to was Communism and specifically the Soviet Union. Today your generation is faced with a different dogma, steeped in deep religious convictions but every bit as deadly to those who oppose them. Education is critical to developing your ability to understand the complex nature of the global, Islamic fundamentalist fascist threat. Manifested in a seemingly undecipherable maze of different groups, organizations, affiliations and sects that comprise this global enemy of freedom and peaceful coexistence between nations, is an enemy who worships death and encourages mothers to strap suicide bomb packs on small children. Make no mistake, this enemy has adherents in almost every country on the planet and is firmly entrenched here at home in America.

I myself have had to go "back to school" in an effort to better understand these proprietors of hate and death for all who choose a different path other than their own twisted vision of a one world Islamic state. Unfortunately, it is a fact that your generation will spend a significant amount of your adult lives dealing with these fanatics. The first step is to arm yourself with knowledge. The internet is a fabulous tool to be used as well as a willingness to invest your time and a few dollars in reading some fabulous books chronicling the history and modern day structure of this enemy. A quick "Google" or browsing the topic of Jihad at Amazon will get you started. The next step is to find the courage to accept the reality of our world and not simply pretend the problem will go away or somebody else will deal with it. Stand up, get involved, speak out and most importantly support those who seek, or are already in, leadership positions who have the courage to address the enemy for who they are and who refuses to bow before the alter of political correctness and appeasement.

> "Those who expect to reap the blessings of freedom, must, like men, undergo the fatigues of supporting it."
>
> *Thomas Paine*

The stakes couldn't be higher. With victory over this Islamofascist enemy comes the freedom and awakening of tens of millions of our fellow man to the reality of an existence driven by the individual's ability to celebrate life, liberty and the pursuit of happiness: key concepts that seem to escape so many who are caught up in our present day sophistication and comfort. Failure, on the other hand, will reap untold misery and hardship. Not just for those who will remain enslaved through ignorance, fear and allegiance to leaders and an ideology whose stated objectives are the destruction of Israel and America and all they stand for, but for your own children and grandchildren who will be left to face a hostile world which will have witnessed the limit of America's power and influence to create a better future for all mankind. That is not a world any of us should like to see. A world where the hope of those not free is extinguished, smothered under a blanket of darkness which man has always seemed so ready and willing to spread over his fellow man. There is a reason that America exists the way she does; that our country has provided a wellspring from which many of mans greatest achievements have flowed; and that is our willingness in the past to recognize common enemies, and make significant and shared sacrifices to defeat them. Nothing less will be required this time and nothing less than our Freedom is at stake.

"Eternal vigilance is the price of Liberty."
Wendell Phillips

Freedom
Action Step Worksheet

Describe what Freedom means to you:

_____

_____

_____

List three things **you will do** to
exercise your Freedom to empower yourself:

_____

_____

_____

*"A person who aims at nothing
is sure to hit it."*

Unkown Author

Focus

F̲ocus is the next of the **8 F's EVERY STUDENT NEEDS**. The main value to you the student in this chapter is found in the fundamental truth that little, if anything, in life can be achieved without having a plan. Now that may sound simplistic and perhaps even silly, but believe me, it is true on so many different levels. This chapter of the Survivor Guide for Student Success will provide a discussion of several critical skills you will need to acquire in order to master the art of staying focused. I recall an old saying from my commodities trading days that directly applies here; "plan your work and work your plan."

> "Concentrate all your thoughts
> upon the work at hand."
> *Alexander Graham Bell*

The first step in creating Focus in your life is to make sure you understand why it is necessary. One perspective is expressed on the opposing page. Another more direct example is embedded in the title of this book... "Success." I'm confident in saying at this point in the book that if you've gotten this far, you are serious about seeking success. Those who aren't stopped a long time ago or perhaps never even turned a page. Regardless, Focus is a key ingredient to success in life, and that's why we're covering it.

The two primary aspects of Focus that you need to know are how to create it and how to maintain it.

> "People with goals succeed because they
> know where they are going...
> it's as simple as that."
>
> *Earl Nightingale*

The process of creating Focus is very straightforward. First establish your goals and then organize the process you intend to follow to achieve them into a plan. Simple enough right? Well, let's break it down a little more and explore both the means of determining and organizing your goals and then the steps involved in creating a path, or plan for you to follow in order to successfully achieve them.

In order to be useful to you here, our discussion of the concept of goals must include the topic of ranking, or your need to make distinctions about the relative importance of multiple goals. For example, the goal of getting an "A" in a particular class as opposed to the goal of a specific over all GPA. Another example could be your goal of attending a social function with a particular individual or getting a summer job. Embedded within these simple examples are two important distinctions for you to recognize. One is the general subject area of your goal or goals, and the other is the degree of generalization of the goals description.

> "The indispensable first step to getting the
> things you want out of life is this;
> decide what you want."
>
> *Ben Stein*

We all have lives that are multifaceted, filled with personal relationships, jobs, education, hobbies and vacations to name but a few components. The trick here is to apply the process your learning about setting goals to each area of your life where you want to focus on accomplishing something specific. In goal setting, specific always trumps general, so the more specific you can break down a general life goal; the better you can create a plan to successfully achieve it.

> "A goal without a plan is just a wish."
> *Antoine de Saint-Exupery*

Once you have identified and prioritized your goals, it is time to build your plan. I should pause here for a moment and deal with a small matter of semantics. While the word "plan" has a generalized, well understood meaning, I want you to always think "plan of action" when you hear or see the word plan. The rationale here is that a plan without action taken to implement it is simply an organized collection of words on paper. Don't forget the action step!!!

> "Plans are only good intentions unless they immediately degenerate into hard work."
> *Peter Drucker*

I have always found the process of building a successful plan an outlet for my more creative side. The reason is that the specific path to successfully achieving any goal has many different potential routes. Your experience, intuition, creativity, sense of adventure and even your willingness to fail (see F#3 / Failure) will all contribute to the selection of specific action steps you will decide to include in your plan for the achievement of a specific goal. Think of the rungs of a ladder as individual steps in your plan. Each one moves you a little closer to your goal.

Some goals require multiple paths that you pursue simultaneously. This often occurs in the case of a more complex goal that requires a plan with multiple components. Timing enters the equation here, in that your action step may require someone else's response in order for you to move forward to the next step in that plan. While waiting for them to act, you can be taking other action on other plan components or for that matter pick up a different plan for another goal you have and work on that.

> "Do not let what you can't do interfere with what you can do."
> *John Wooden*

The last thing to be said here about goals and planning as tools to help you create and maintain Focus in your life is that things change and you need to be prepared to change as well. A great planner allows for his/her plan to be modified. Adapt to new circumstances or obstacles that will appear. No one can predict the future but you can always choose how you will react to it.

Focus
Action Step Worksheet

List three areas of your life that can benefit from more Focus:

_____

_____

_____

List three things **you will do** to
create more Focus in your life:

_____

_____

_____

"My will shall shape the future.
Whether I fail or succeed shall be no
man's doing but my own.

I am the force; I can clear any obstacle
before me or I can be lost in the maze.

My choice; my responsibility; win or
lose, only I hold the key to my destiny."

Elaine Maxwell

Future

Future is the last of the **8 F'S EVERY STUDENT NEEDS.**
Congratulations !!! You've almost made it to the end of the
Survivor Guide for Student Success. In this last chapter I want
to reinforce some of the central themes and concepts we've
already covered but now within the context of your Future.
It is my hope and prayer for each of you at this point that
you have found at least one thing within these pages that will
make a difference in your life going forward. That is after
all, the goal I set for myself when I undertook this effort; to
positively impact peoples lives through sharing my thoughts
as they have been influenced by my experience on September
11, 2001.

> "In times of change, learners inherit the Earth, while
> the learned find themselves beautifully equipped to
> deal with a world that no longer exists."
>
> *Eric Hoffer*

The future, at least in specific details is typically considered
unknowable, and for the most part I would concur with this
assessment. Where I would differ is in the broader perspective
that could be illustrated by accepting for the moment the prem-
ise that change is guaranteed to be a big part of your future.
And not just significant personal change, as you move more
fully into adulthood, but global political, sociological, envi-
ronmental and technological change. What you will require is
an ability to adapt and apply not just what you have learned,

but more importantly the process by which you have learned it. Staying engaged with your need for learning will serve you throughout your lifetime. Stay curious, ask why, investigate for yourself and nurture your skills of critical examination.

> "The best thing about the future
> is that it only comes one day at a time."
>
> *Abraham Lincoln*

Often when we face changes in our lives we can't help but feel a little less in control. This can be accompanied by a sense of being overwhelmed, especially if the pace of change has been rapid, or several unrelated changes occur at or around the same time. I'm reminded of something my Dad often told me when I faced events or change that made me feel this way and I want to offer it now to you; "keep it in perspective" he would tell me. I'm sure I didn't always implement this sage wisdom but looking back, it is in fact very good advice. Most things become clearer to us with the passage of a little time. Sometimes just "sleeping" on an issue overnight will allow for a clearer, more insightful perspective as early as the next morning. Don't be in to big of a hurry to make adjustments to changes that come your way. Think things through and recognize that everyone else is meeting their future at exactly the same pace as you.

> "The future is something which everyone
> reaches at the rate of sixty minutes an hour,
> whatever they do, whoever they are."
>
> *C.S. Lewis*

Another important component of the **8 F'S EVERY STUDENT NEEDS** that I want to specifically address with regard to your Future is the issue of adversity. So much of your success in life depends upon the mental attitude you adopt in facing life's roadblocks. It is important to recognize that this applies equally to both obstacles you encounter and overcome along the way, and the outright failures you will experience when you've been knocked down and find yourself needing to stand up, dust yourself off and take a fresh start toward your goal.

You must build and nurture a positive self image, seeing yourself in your mind's eye as being successful, accomplishing your goal. These mental skills are critically important to develop and must be exercised or practiced regularly in order that they become second nature to you. Is this easy? NO ! Is this worth the effort to fight back against the all too natural instinct of giving up, telling yourself something's are just too hard? YES ! All you need is the courage to hold a strong inner belief in yourself and your ability to survive and overcome life's challenges.

> "Courage, it would seem, is nothing less than the power to overcome danger, misfortune, fear, injustice, while continuing to affirm inwardly that life with all its sorrows is good."
>
> *Dorothy Thompson*

I want to close out this discussion of your Future by sharing with you two perspectives that are perfectly captured in the quotations I've included below. The first is in recognition that our future is not something that can be perfectly planned for, spotted on the horizon and methodically reached. Life seems to be more like a wire spring where it remains coiled for long periods of time with seemingly little movement when suddenly and often unexpectedly, it leaps forward releasing its energy. Your journey to your future will undoubtedly catch you off guard at times. Remember to smile and enjoy the ride!

> "The future has a way of arriving unannounced."
> *George Will*

Lastly, I want to thank you for allowing me to share my thoughts with you and I commend you for undertaking the task of reading the Survivor Guide for Student Success.

If I've been successful, you should feel empowered to meet your future with confidence, determination and a rock solid belief in yourself and your ability to succeed. Review the action steps you completed throughout the book and make them part of your daily routine. Practice positive "self talk" and let yourself know that you believe in you. Most of all recognize that it is now, this very moment, that you can start your life journey anew with new found confidence and a stronger sense of purpose than ever before.

> "Now is the accepted time, not tomorrow, not some more convenient season. It is today that our best work can be done and not some future day or future year. It is today that we fit ourselves for the greater usefulness of tomorrow."
> *E.B. Du Bois*

Future
Action Step Worksheet

List three things you would like
to make a part of your Future:

_____

_____

_____

List three things **you will do** to
make your Future a reality:

_____

_____

_____